P

Pocket Reference

Clinton Wong

O'REILLY®

Beijing • Cambridge • Farnham • Köln • Paris • Sebastopol • Taipei • Tokyo

HTTP Pocket Reference

by Clinton Wong

Street,

May 2000:   First Edition.

Library of Congress Cataloging-in-Publication Data

Wong, Clinton.
    HTTP pocket reference /Clinton Wong. p. cm.
    ISBN 1-56592-862-8
    1. Hypertext systems. 2. HTTP (Computer network protocol)
        I. Title.

QA76.76.H94 W66 2000
005.7'2--dc21   00-032654

1-56592-862-8   [10/00]
[C]

Table of Contents

What Is HTTP? 1

HTTP Transactions 2

Client Methods 10

Server Response Codes 22

Headers 31

URL Encoding 51

Client and Server Identification 55

Referring Documents 55

Retrieving Content 56

Media Types 58

Cookies 68

Authorization 69

Persistent Connections 72

Client Caching 73

HTTP Pocket Reference

This book describes HTTP, the Hypertext Transfer Protocol. It provides a high level description of how the protocol works, along with reference information on client requests and server responses. Included are dumps of HTTP transactions, as well as tabular data that summarizes most of the standardized parameters used in HTTP.

The HTTP Pocket Reference is intended for system administrators, web site developers, and software engineers. With an understanding of HTTP, system administrators will have a better understanding of web site configuration and debugging. Web site designers can implement services that make better use of the protocol and streamline web client and server interaction. Software engineers who need to implement HTTP will find this book useful for its short, concise description of the protocol.

What Is HTTP?

HTTP is the protocol behind the World Wide Web. With every web transaction, HTTP is invoked. HTTP is behind every request for a web document or graphic, every click of a hypertext link, and every submission of a form. The Web is about distributing information over the Internet, and HTTP is the protocol used to do so.

HTTP is useful because it provides a standardized way for computers to communicate with each other. HTTP specifies how clients request data, and how servers respond to these requests. By understanding how HTTP works, you'll be able to:

- Manually query web servers and receive low-level information that typical web browsers hide from the user. With this information, you can better understand the configuration and capabilities of a particular server, and debug configuration errors with the server or programming errors in programs invoked by the web server.

- Understand the interaction between web clients (browsers, robots, search engines, etc.) and web servers.

- Streamline web services to make better use of the protocol.

HTTP Transactions

This section presents an example of a common web transaction, showing the HTTP exchanged between the client and server program.

Requests

Given the following URL:

```
http://hypothetical.ora.com:80/
```

The browser interprets the URL as follows:

http://
> Use HTTP, the Hypertext Transfer Protocol.

hypothetical.ora.com
> Contact a computer over the network with the hostname of *hypothetical.ora.com.*

:80
> Connect to the computer at port 80. The port number can be any legitimate IP port number: 1 through 65535, inclusively.* If the colon and port number are omitted, the port number is assumed to be HTTP's default port number, which is 80.

/

> Anything after the hostname and optional port number is regarded as a document path. In this example, the document path is /.

---

* Assuming IP version 4 addressing, which is the most common version of IP currently in use.

So the browser connects to *hypothetical.ora.com* on port 80 using the HTTP protocol. The message that the browser sends to the server is:

```
GET / HTTP/1.1
Accept: image/gif, image/x-xbitmap, image/
    jpeg, image/pjpeg, */*
Accept-Language: en-us
Accept-Encoding: gzip, deflate
User-Agent: Mozilla/4.0 (compatible; MSIE
    5.01; Windows NT)
Host: hypothetical.ora.com
Connection: Keep-Alive
```

Let's look at what these lines are saying:

1. The first line of this request (`GET / HTTP/1.1`) requests a document at / from the server. `HTTP/1.1` is given as the version of the HTTP protocol that the browser uses.

2. The second line tells the server what kind of documents are accepted by the browser.

3. The third line indicates that the preferred language is English. This header allows the client to specify a preference for one or more languages, in the event that a server has the same document in multiple languages.

4. The fourth line indicates that the client understands how to interpret a server response that is compressed with the gzip or deflate algorithm.

5. In the fifth line, beginning with the string `User-Agent`, the client identifies itself as Mozilla version 4.0, running on Windows NT. In parenthesis it mentions that it is really Microsoft Internet Explorer version 5.01.

6. The sixth line tells the server what the client thinks the server's hostname is. This header is mandatory in HTTP 1.1, but optional in HTTP 1.0. Since the server may have multiple hostnames, the client indicates which hostname is being requested. In this environment, a web server can have a different document tree for each hostname assigned to it. If the client hasn't specified the server's

hostname, the server may be unable to determine which document tree to use.

7. The seventh line (Connection:) tells the server to keep the TCP connection open until explicitly told to disconnect. Under HTTP 1.1, the default server behavior is to keep the connection open until the client specifies that the connection should be closed. The standard behavior in HTTP 1.0 is to close the connection after the client's request. See the discussion under "Persistent Connections" later in this book for details.

Together, these seven lines constitute a *request*. Lines two through seven are *request headers*. The section "Headers" discusses each header in more detail.

Responses

Given a request like the one previously shown, the server looks for the server resource associated with "/" and returns it to the browser, preceding it with header information in its response. The resource associated with the URL depends on how the server is implemented. It could be a static file or it could be dynamically generated. In this case, the server returns:

```
HTTP/1.1 200 OK
Date: Mon, 06 Dec 1999 20:54:26 GMT
Server: Apache/1.3.6 (Unix)
Last-Modified: Fri, 04 Oct 1996 14:06:11 GMT
ETag: "2f5cd-964-381e1bd6"
Accept-Ranges: bytes
Content-length: 327
Connection: close
Content-type: text/html

<title>Sample Homepage</title>
<img src="/images/oreilly_mast.gif">
<h1>Welcome</h1>
```

```
Hi there, this is a simple web page. Granted,
it may not be as elegant as some other web
pages you've seen on the net, but there are
some common qualities:

<ul>
  <li> An image,
  <li> Text,
  <li> and a <a href="/example2.html">
hyperlink. </a>
</ul>
```

If you look at this response, you'll see it begins with a
series of lines that specify information about the document
and about the server itself. After a blank line, it returns the
document. Lines 2–9 are called the *response header*, and
the part after the first blank line is called the *body* or *entity,* or *entity-body.* Let's look at the header information:

1. The first line, HTTP/1.1 200 OK, tells the client what
   version of the HTTP protocol the server uses. But more
   importantly, by returning a status code of 200, it says
   that the document has been found and will transmit the
   document in its response.

2. The second line indicates the current date on the server.
   The time is expressed in Greenwich Mean Time (GMT).

3. The third line tells the client what kind of software the
   server is running. In this case, the server is Apache
   version 1.3.6 on Unix.

4. The fourth line specifies the most recent modification
   time of the document requested by the client. This
   modification time is often used for caching purposes—
   so a browser may not need to request the entire HTML
   file again if its modification time doesn't change

5. The fifth line indicates an entity tag. This provides the
   web client with a unique identifier for the server
   resource. It is highly unlikely for two different server

---

resources to have the same entity tag. This tag provides a powerful mechanism for caching.

6. The sixth line indicates to the browser that the server possesses the ability to return subsections of a document, instead of returning the entire document every time it is requested. This is useful for retrieving records in a document, which may be useful for database and streaming multimedia applications.

7. The seventh line tells the client how many bytes are in the entity body that follow the headers. In this case, the entity body is 327 bytes long.

8. The eighth line indicates that the connection will close after the server's response. If the client wants to send another request, it will need to open another connection to the server.

9. The ninth line (Content-type) tells the browser what kind of document the server is including in its response. In this case, it's HTML.

After all this information, a blank line and the document text follow. Figure 1 shows the transaction.

Parsing the HTML

The document is in HTML (as promised in the Content-type line). The browser retrieves the document and then formats it as needed—for example, each <li> item between the <ul> and </ul> is printed as a bullet and indented, the <img> tag displays a graphic on the screen, etc.

To process the image tag, the browser actually initiates a second HTTP request to retrieve the image. When the server returns the image, it includes a Content-type header indicating the format of the image (e.g., image/gif). From the declared content type, the browser knows what kind of image it will receive and can render it as required. The

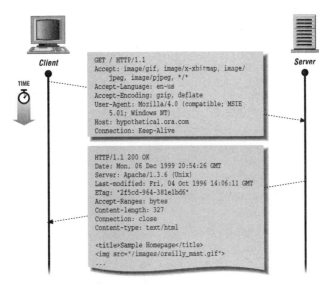

Figure 1. A simple transaction

browser shouldn't guess the content type based on the document path; it is up to the server to tell the client.

The important thing to note is that the HTML formatting and image rendering are done at the browser end. All the server does is return documents; the browser is responsible for how they look to the user.

Structure of HTTP Transactions

To generalize, all client requests and server responses follow the same general structure shown in Figure 1.

Figure 2 shows the structure of a client request.

HTTP transactions do not need to use all the headers. As a matter of fact, it is possible to perform some HTTP requests without supplying any header information at all. For example, in the most simple case, a request of GET / HTTP/1.0

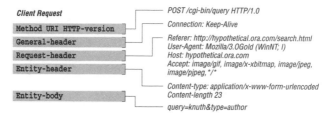

Figure 2. Structure of a client request

without any headers is sufficient for most servers to understand the client.*

HTTP requests have the following general components:

1. The first line tells the client which *method* to use, which
   entity (document) to apply it to, and which version of
   HTTP the client is using. Possible HTTP 1.1 methods are
   GET, POST, HEAD, PUT, LINK, UNLINK, DELETE,
   OPTIONS, and TRACE. HTTP 1.0 does not support the
   OPTIONS or TRACE method. Not all methods need be
   supported by a server.

   The URL specifies the location of a document to apply the
   method to. Each server may have its own way of translat-
   ing the URL string into some form of usable resource. For
   example, the URL may represent a document to transmit
   to the client. Or the URL may actually map to a program,
   the output of which is sent to the client.

   Finally, the last entry on the first line specifies the version of HTTP the client is using.

2. General message headers are optional headers used in
   both the client request and server response. They indicate
   general information such as the current time or the path
   through a network that the client and server are using.

---

* Use of HTTP 1.1 is encourage over 1.0. In the case of HTTP 1.1, a
  GET / HTTP/1.1 with a Host header is the minimal amount of
  information needed for an HTTP 1.1 request.

---

3. Request headers tell the server more information about the client. The client can identify itself and the user to the server, and specify preferred document formats that it would like to see from the server.

4. Entity headers are used when an entity (a document) is about to be sent. They specify information about the entity, such as encoding schemes, length, type, and origin.

Now for server responses. Figure 3 maps out the structure of a server response.

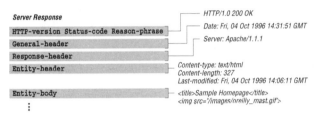

Figure 3. Structure of a server response

In the server response, the general header and entity headers are the same as those used in the client request. The entity-body is like the one used in the client request, except that it is used as a response.

The first part of the first line indicates the version of HTTP the server is using. The server will make every attempt to conform to the most compatible version of HTTP that the client is using. The status code indicates the result of the request, and the reason phrase is a human-readable description of the status code.

The response header tells the client about the configuration of the server. It informs the client of the methods that are supported, requests authorization, or tells the client to try again later.

Client Methods

A client request method is a *command* or *request* that a web client issues to a server. You can think of the method as the declaration of the client's intentions. There are exceptions, of course, but here are some generalizations:

- You can think of a GET request as meaning that you just want to retrieve a resource on the server. This resource could be the contents of a static file or invoke a program that generates data.

- A HEAD request means that you just want some information about the document, but don't need the document itself.

- A POST request says that you're providing some information of your own (generally used for fill-in forms). This typically changes the state of the server in some way. For example, it could create a record in a database.

- PUT is used to provide a new or replacement document to be stored on the server.

- DELETE is used to remove a document on the server.

- TRACE asks that proxies declare themselves in the headers, so the client can learn the path that the document took (and thus determine where something might have been garbled or lost). This is used for protocol debugging purposes.

- OPTIONS is used when the client wants to know what other methods can be used for that document (or for the server at large).

- CONNECT is used when a client needs to talk to a HTTPS server through a proxy server.

Other HTTP methods that you may see (LINK, UNLINK, and PATCH) are less clearly defined.

GET: Retrieve a Document

The GET method requests a document from a specific location on the server. This is the main method used for
document retrieval. The response to a GET request can be
generated by the server in many ways. For example, the
response could come from:

- A file accessible by the web server

- The output of a CGI script or server extension language
  like NSAPI, ISAPI, Apache modules, Java Server Pages,
  Active Server Pages, etc.

- The result of a server computation, for instance real-time
  decompression of online files

- Information obtained from a hardware device, such as a
  video camera

After the client uses the GET method in its request, the
server responds with a status line, headers, and data
requested by the client. If the server cannot process the
request, due to an error or lack of authorization, the server
usually sends an explanation in the entity-body of the
response.

For example:

```
GET / HTTP/1.1
Accept: image/gif, image/x-xbitmap,
    image/jpeg, image/pjpeg, */*
Accept-Language: en-us
Accept-Encoding: gzip, deflate
User-Agent: Mozilla/4.0 (compatible; MSIE
    5.01; Windows NT)
Host: hypothetical.ora.com
Connection: Keep-Alive
```

The server responds with:

```
HTTP/1.1 200 OK
Date: Mon, 06 Dec 1999 20:54:26 GMT
Server: Apache/1.3.6 (Unix)
Last-Modified: Fri, 04 Oct 1996 14:06:11 GMT
```

```
ETag: "2f5cd-964-381e1bd6"
Accept-Ranges: bytes
Content-length: 327
Connection: close
Content-Type: text/html

(body of document here)
```

HEAD: Retrieve Header Information

The HEAD method is functionally like GET, except that the server replies with a response line and headers, but no entity-body. The headers returned by the server with the HEAD method should be exactly the same as the headers returned with a GET request. This method is often used by web clients to verify the document's existence or properties (like `Content-length` or `Content-type`), but the client has no intention of retrieving the document in the transaction. Many applications exist for the HEAD method, which make it possible to retrieve:

- Modification time of a document for caching purposes

- Size of the document, to do page layout, estimate arrival time, or skip the document and retrieve a smaller version of the document

- Type of the document, to allow the client to examine only documents of a certain type

- Type of server, to allow customized server queries

It is important to note that most of the header information provided by a server is optional, and may not be given by all servers.

For example:

```
GET / HTTP/1.1
Accept: image/gif, image/x-xbitmap,
    image/jpeg, image/pjpeg, */*
Accept-Language: en-us
Accept-Encoding: gzip, deflate
User-Agent: Mozilla/4.0 (compatible; MSIE
```

```
    5.01; Windows NT)
 Host: hypothetical.ora.com
 Connection: Keep-Alive
```

The server responds with:

```
HTTP/1.1 200 OK
Date: Mon, 06 Dec 1999 20:54:26 GMT
Server: Apache/1.3.6 (Unix)
Last-Modified: Fri, 04 Oct 1996 14:06:11 GMT
ETag: "2f5cd-964-381e1bd6"
Accept-Ranges: bytes
Content-length: 327
Connection: close
Content-type: text/html
```

Note the server does not return any data after the headers.

POST: Send Data to the Server

The POST method allows the client to specify data to be
sent to some data-handling program that the server can
access. It can be used for many applications. For example,
POST could be used to provide input for:

- CGI programs

- Gateways to network services, like an NNTP server

- Command-line interface programs

- Annotation of documents on the server

- Database operations

In practice, POST is used with CGI programs that happen
to interface with other resources like network services and
command-line programs. In the future, POST may be
directly interfaced with a wider variety of server resources.

In a POST request, the data sent to the server is in the entity-
body of the client's request. After the server processes the
POST request and headers, it may pass the entity-body to
another program (specified by the URL) for processing. In
some cases, a server's custom API may handle the data,
instead of a program external to the server.

POST requests should be accompanied by a Content-type header, describing the format of the client's entity-body. The most commonly used format with POST is the URL-encoding scheme used for CGI applications. It allows form data to be translated into a list of variables and values. Browsers that support forms send the data in URL-encoded format. For example, given the HTML form of:

```
<title>Create New Account</title>
<center><hr><h1>Account Creation Form</h1><hr>
</center>
<form method="post" action="/cgi-bin/
create.pl">
<pre>
<b>
Enter user name: <INPUT NAME="user"
MAXLENGTH="20" SIZE="20">
Password: <INPUT NAME="pass1" TYPE="password"
 MAXLENGTH="20" SIZE="20">
(Type it again to verify) <INPUT NAME="pass2"
TYPE="password"
 MAXLENGTH="20" SIZE="20">
</b>
</pre>
<INPUT TYPE="submit" VALUE="Create account">
<input type="reset" value="Start over">
</form>
```

Let's insert some values and submit the form. As the user-name, util-tester was entered. For the password, 1234 was entered (twice). Upon submission, the client sends:

```
POST /cgi-bin/create.pl  HTTP/1.1
Host: examples.ora.com
Referer: http://examples.ora.com/create.html
Accept: image/gif, image/x-xbitmap,
    image/jpeg, image/pjpeg, */*
Content-type: application/x-www-form-
    urlencoded
Content-length: 38

user=util-tester&pass1=1234&pass2=1234
```

Now the variables defined in the form have been associated with the values entered by the user. This information is then passed to the server in URL-encoded format, which is described below.

The server determines that the client used a POST method, processes the URL, executes the program associated with the URL, and pipes the client's entity-body to a program specified at the address of */cgi-bin/create.pl*. The server maps this "web address" to the location of a program, usually in a designated CGI directory (in this case, */cgi-bin*). The CGI program then interprets the input as CGI data, decodes the entity body, processes it, and returns a response entity-body to the client:

```
HTTP/1.0 200 OK
Date: Sat, 20-May-95 03:25:12 GMT
Server: NCSA/1.3
MIME-version: 1.0
Content-type: text/html
Last-modified: Wed, 14-Mar-95 18:15:23 GMT
Content-length: 95

<title>User Created</title>
<h1>The util-tester account has been created
</h1>
```

URL-encoded format

Using the POST method is not the only way that forms send information. Forms can also use the GET method, and append the URL-encoded data to the URL, following a question mark. If the `<form>` tag had contained the line `method="get"` instead of `method="post"`, the request would have looked like this:

```
GET /cgi-bin/create.pl?user=util-
    tester&pass1=1234&pass2=1234 HTTP/1.1
Host: examples.ora.com
Referer: http://examples.ora.com/create.html
Accept: image/gif, image/x-xbitmap,
    image/jpeg, image/pjpeg, */*
```

This is one reason that the data sent by a CGI program is in a special format: since it can be appended to the URL itself, it cannot contain special characters such as spaces, new-lines, etc. For that reason, it is called *URL-encoded*.

The URL-encoded format, identified with a `Content-type` of *application/x-www-form-urlencoded* format by clients, is composed of a single line with variable names and values concatenated together. The variable and value are separated by an equal sign (=), and each variable/value pair is separated by an ampersand symbol (&). In the example given above, there are three variables: `user`, `pass1`, and `pass2`. The values (respectively) are: `util-tester`, `1234`, and `1234`. The encoding looks like this:

```
user=util-tester&pass1=1234&pass2=1234
```

When the client wants to send characters that normally have special meanings, like the ampersand and equal sign, the client replaces the characters with a percent sign (%) followed by an ASCII value in hexadecimal (base 16). This removes ambiguity when a special character is used. The only exception, however, is the space character (ASCII 32), which can be encoded as a plus sign (+) as well as `%20`. The preferred format is `%20` instead of the plus sign.

When the server retrieves information from a form, the server passes it to a CGI program, which then decodes it from URL-encoded format to retrieve the values entered by the user.

File uploads with POST

POST isn't limited to the *application/x-www-form-urlencoded* content type. Consider the following HTML:

```
<form method="post" action="post.pl"
enctype="multipart/form-data">
Enter a file to upload:<br>
<input name="thefile" type="file"><br>
<input name="done" type="submit">
</form>
```

This form allows the user to select a file and upload it to the server. Notice that the <form> tag contains an enctype attribute, specifying an encoding type of *multipart/form-data* instead of the default, *application/x-www-form-urlencoded*. This encoding type will be used by the browser as the content type when the form is submitted. As an example, suppose I create a file called *hi.txt* with the contents "hi there" and put it in *c:/temp/*. I use the HTML form to include the file and then hit the submit button. My browser sends this:

```
POST /cgi-bin/post.pl HTTP/1.0
Referer: http://hypothetical.ora.com/clinton/
upload.html
Connection: Keep-Alive
User-Agent: Mozilla/3.01Gold (WinNT; U)
Host: hypothetical.ora.com
Accept: image/gif, image/x-xbitmap, image/
jpeg, image/pjpeg, */*
Content-type: multipart/form-data; boundary=--
------------------------11512135131576
Content-Length: 313

----------------------------11512135131576
Content-Disposition: form-data; name="done"

Submit Query
----------------------------11512135131576
Content-Disposition: form-data;
name="thefile"; filename="c:\temp\hi.txt"
Content-Type: text/plain

hi there

----------------------------11512135131576--
```

The entity-body of the request is a multipart Multipurpose Internet Mail Extensions (MIME) message. See RFC 1867 for more details.

PUT: Store the Entity-Body at the URL

When a client uses the PUT method, it requests that the included entity-body should be stored on the server at the requested URL. With HTML editors, it is possible to publish documents onto the server with a PUT method. Given an HTML editor with some sample HTML in the editor, suppose the user saves the document in *C:\temp\example.html* and publishes it to *http://publish.ora.com/example.htm*.

When the user presses the OK button, the client contacts *publish.ora.com* at port 80 and then sends:

```
PUT /example.html HTTP/1.1
Host: publish.ora.com
Pragma: no-cache
Connection: close
User-Agent: SimplePublish/1.0
Accept: image/gif, image/x-xbitmap,
    image/jpeg, image/pjpeg, */*
Content-type: text/html
Content-Length: 182

<!DOCTYPE HTML PUBLIC "-//W3C//DTD HTML 3.2//
EN">
<HTML>
<HEAD>
    <TITLE></TITLE>
</HEAD>
<BODY>

<H2>This is a header</H2>

<P>This is a simple html document.</P>

</BODY>
</HTML>
```

The server stores the client's entity-body at */example.html* and then responds with:

```
HTTP/1.0 201 Created
Date: Fri, 04 Oct 1996 14:31:51 GMT
```

```
Server: HypotheticalPublish/1.0
Content-type: text/html
Content-length: 30

<h1>The file was created.</h1>
```

In practice, a web server may request authorization from
the client. Most webmasters won't allow any arbitrary client to publish documents on the server. When prompted
with an "authorization denied" response code, the browser
will typically ask the user to enter relevant authorization
information. After receiving the information from the user,
the browser retransmits the request with additional headers
that describe the authorization information.

It should be noted that some publishing applications forget
to include a `Content-type` in the PUT request. This does
not conform to the HTTP specification, but workarounds in
some server software may exist for it.

DELETE: Remove URL

Since PUT creates new URLs on the server, it seems appropriate to have a mechanism to delete URLs as well. The
DELETE method does what you think it would do.

A client request might read:

```
DELETE /images/logo22.gif HTTP/1.1
Host: hypothetical.ora.com
```

The server responds with a success code upon success:

```
HTTP/1.0 200 OK
Date: Fri, 04 Oct 1996 14:31:51 GMT
Server: HypotheticalPublish/1.0
Content-type: text/html
Content-length: 21

<h1>URL deleted.</h1>
```

Needless to say, any server that supports the DELETE method is likely to request authorization before carrying through with the request.

TRACE: View the Client's Message Through the Request Chain

The TRACE method allows a programmer to see how the client's message is modified as it passes through a series of proxy servers. The recipient of a TRACE method echoes the HTTP request headers back to the client. When the TRACE method is used with the Max-Forwards and Via headers, a client can determine the chain of intermediate proxy servers between the original client and web server. The Max-Forwards request header specifies the number of intermediate proxy servers allowed to pass the request. Each proxy server decrements the Max-Forwards value and appends its HTTP version number and hostname to the Via header. A proxy server that receives a Max-Forwards value of 0 returns the client's HTTP headers as an entity-body with the Content-type of *message/http*. This feature resembles *traceroute*, a UNIX program used to identify routers between two machines in an IP-based network. HTTP clients do not send an entity-body when issuing a TRACE request.

Figure 4 shows the progress of a TRACE request. After the client makes the request, the first proxy server receives the request, decrements the Max-Forwards value by one, adds itself to a Via header, and forwards it to the second proxy server. The second proxy server receives the request, adds itself to the Via header, and sends the request back, since Max-Forwards is now 0 (zero).

OPTIONS: Request Other Options Available for the URL

When a client request contains the OPTIONS method, it requests a list of options for a particular resource on the

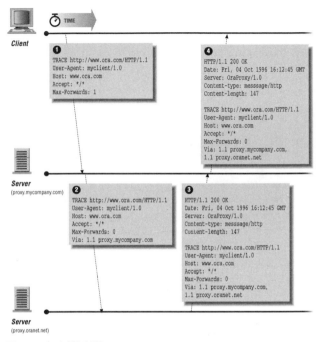

Figure 4. A TRACE request

server. The client specifies a URL for the OPTIONS method, or an asterisk (*) to refer to the entire server. The server then responds with a list of request methods or other options that are valid for the requested resource, using the Allow header for an individual resource, or the Public header for the entire server. Figure 5 shows an example of the OPTIONS method in action.

CONNECT: Proxy Access to Secure Web Servers

When an http client wants to connect to an HTTPS server, but needs to do it through a proxy server, it issues a CONNECT

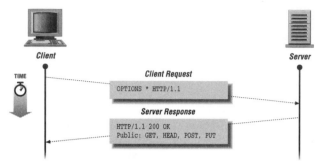

Figure 5. An OPTIONS request

to the proxy server. For example, the client connects to the proxy server and issues:

```
CONNECT www.onsale.com:443 HTTP/1.0
User-Agent: Mozilla/4.08 [en] (WinNT; U ;Nav)
```

And the server responds with:

```
HTTP/1.0 200 Connection established
Proxy-agent: Apache/1.3.9 (Unix)
```

From there, all traffic is encrypted with SSL. The browser sends another HTTP message, this time inside the connection that was established with CONNECT through the proxy server. At this point, the proxy server just relays the data between the client and origin server.

Server Response Codes

The initial line of the server's response indicates the HTTP version, a three-digit status code, and a human-readable description of the result. Status codes are grouped as follows:

Code Range	Response Meaning
100–199	Informational
200–299	Client request successful

Code Range	Response Meaning
300–399	Client request redirected, further action necessary
400–499	Client request incomplete
500–599	Server errors

HTTP defines only a few specific codes in each range, although these ranges will become more populated as HTTP evolves.

If a client receives a response code that it does not recognize, it should understand its basic meaning from its numerical range. While most web browsers handle codes in the 100, 200, and 300 ranges silently, some error codes in the 400 and 500 ranges are commonly reported back to the user (e.g., "404 Not Found").

Informational (100 Range)

Previous to HTTP 1.1, the 100 range of status codes was left undefined. In HTTP 1.1, the 100 range was defined for the server to declare that it is ready for the client to continue with a request, or to declare that it will be switching to another protocol.

The status codes currently defined are:

Code	Meaning
100 Continue	The initial part of the request has been received, and the client may continue with its request.
101 Switching Protocols	The server is complying with a client request to switch protocols to the one specified in the `Upgrade` header field.

Client Request Successful (200 Range)

The most common response for a successful HTTP transaction is 200 (OK), indicating that the client's request was successful, and the server's response contains the request data. If the request was a GET method, the requested information is returned in the response data section. The HEAD method is honored by returning header information about the URL. The POST method is honored by executing the POST data handler and returning a resulting entity-body.

The following is a complete list of successful response codes:

Code	Meaning
200 OK	The client's request was successful, and the server's response contains the requested data.
201 Created	This status code is used whenever a new URL is created. With this result code, the Location header is given by the server to specify where the new data was placed.
202 Accepted	The request was accepted but not immediately acted upon. More information about the transaction may be given in the entity-body of the server's response. There is no guarantee that the server will actually honor the request, even though it may seem like a legitimate request at the time of acceptance.
203 Non-Authoritative Information	The information in the entity header is from a local or third-party copy, not from the original server.

Code	Meaning
204 No Content	A status code and header are given in the response, but there is no entity-body in the reply. Browsers should not update their document view upon receiving this response. This is a useful code for CGI programs to use when they accept data from a form but want the browser view to stay at the form.
205 Reset Content	The browser should clear the form used for this transaction for additional input. For data-entry CGI applications.
206 Partial Content	The server is returning partial data of the size requested. Used in response to a request specifying a `Range` header. The server must specify the range included in the response with the `Content-Range` header.

Redirection (300 Range)

When a document has moved, the server might be configured to tell clients where it has been moved. Clients can then retrieve the new URL silently, without the user knowing. Presumably the client may want to know whether the move is a permanent one or not, so there are a few common response codes for moved documents: 301 (Moved Permanently), 302 (Found), and 307 (Temporary Redirect).

Ideally, a 301 code would indicate to the client that, from now on, requests for this URL should be sent directly to the new one, thus avoiding unnecessary transactions in the future. Think of it like a change of address card from a friend; the post office is nice enough to forward your mail to your friend's new address for the next year, but it's better to get used to the new address so your mail will get to her faster, and won't start getting returned someday.

A 302 or 307 code, on the other hand, just says that the document has moved but will return. If a 301 is a change of address card, a 302 or 307 is a note on your friend's door saying she's gone to the movies. Either way, the client should request the new URL specified by the server in the Location header, but continue to go to the original URL in the future.

The following is a complete list of redirection status codes:

Code	Meaning
300 Multiple Choices	The requested URL refers to more than one resource. For example, the URL could refer to a document that has been translated into many languages. The entity-body returned by the server could have a list of more specific data about how to choose the correct resource. The client should allow the user to select from the list of URLs returned by the server, where appropriate.
301 Moved Permanently	The requested URL is no longer used by the server, and the operation specified in the request was not performed. The new location for the requested document is specified in the Location header. All future requests for the document should use the new URL.
302 Found	This status code is deprecated, and serves the same purpose as status code 307.
303 See Other	The requested URL can be found at a different URL (specified in the Location header) and should be retrieved by a GET on that resource.
304 Not Modified	This is the response code to an If-Modified-Since or If-None-Match header, where the URL has not been modified since the specified date. The entity-body is not sent, and the client should use its own local copy.

Code	Meaning
305 Use Proxy	The requested URL must be accessed through the proxy in the `Location` header.
307 Moved Temporarily	The requested URL has moved, but only temporarily. The `Location` header specifies the new location, but no information is given about the validity of the redirect in the future. The client should revisit the original URL in the future.

Client Request Incomplete (400 Range)

Sometimes the server just can't process the request. Either something was wrong with the document or with the request itself. By far, the server status code that web users are most familiar with is 404 (Not Found), the code returned when the requested document does not exist. This isn't because it's the most common code that servers return, but because it's one of the few codes that the client passes to the user rather than intercepting and handling it in its own way.

For example, when the server sends a 401 (Unauthorized) code, the client does not pass the code directly to the user. Instead, it triggers the client to prompt the user for a username and password, and then resend the request with that information supplied. With the 401 status code, the server supplies the `WWW-Authenticate` header to specify the authentication scheme and realm it needs authorization for, and the client returns the username and password for that scheme and realm in the `Authorization` header.

When testing clients you have written yourself, watch out for code 400 (Bad Request), indicating a syntax error in your client's request, and code 405 (Method Not Allowed), which declares that the method the client used for the document is not valid. (Along with the 405 code, the server sends an Allow header, listing the accepted methods for the document.)

The 408 (Request Time-out) code means that the client's request wasn't completed, and the server gave up waiting for the client to finish. A client might receive this code if it did not supply the entity-body properly, or (under HTTP 1.1) if it neglected to supply a Connection: Close header.

The following is a complete listing of status codes implying that the client's request was faulty:

Code	Meaning
400 Bad Request	This response code indicates that the server detected a syntax error in the client's request.
401 Unauthorized	The result code is given along with the WWW-Authenticate header to indicate that the request lacked proper authorization, and the client should supply proper authorization when requesting this URL again. See the description of the Authorization header for more information on how authorization works in HTTP.
402 Payment Required	This code is not yet implemented in HTTP.
403 Forbidden	The request was denied for a reason the server does not want to (or has no means to) indicate to the client.
404 Not Found	The document at the specified URL does not exist.
405 Method Not Allowed	This code is given with the Allow header and indicates that the method used by the client is not supported for this URL.

Code	Meaning
406 Not Acceptable	The URL specified by the client exists, but not in a format preferred by the client. Along with this code, the server provides the `Content-Language`, `Content-Encoding`, and `Content-type` headers.
407 Proxy Authentica-tion Required	The proxy server needs to authorize the request before forwarding it. Used with the `Proxy-Authenticate` header.
408 Request Time-out	This response code means the client did not produce a full request within some predetermined time (usually specified in the server's configuration), and the server is disconnecting the network connection.
409 Conflict	This code indicates that the request conflicts with another request or with the server's configuration. Information about the conflict should be returned in the data portion of the reply. For example, this response code could be given when a client's request would cause integrity problems in a database.
410 Gone	This code indicates that the requested URL no longer exists and has been permanently removed from the server.
411 Length Required	The server will not accept the request without a `Content-length` header supplied in the request.
412 Precon-dition Failed	The condition specified by one or more `If...` headers in the request evaluated to false.
413 Request Entity Too Large	The server will not process the request because its entity-body is too large.

Code	Meaning
414 Request URL Too Long	The server will not process the request because its request URL is too large.
415 Unsupported Media Type	The server will not process the request because its entity-body is in an unsupported format.
416 Request Range Not Satisfiable	The requested byte range is not available and is out of bounds.
417 Expectation Failed	The server is unable to meet the demands of the Expect header given by the client.

Server Error (500 Range)

Occasionally, the error might be with the server itself—or, more commonly, with the CGI portion of the server. CGI programmers are painfully familiar with the 500 (Internal Server Error) code, which frequently means that their program crashed. One error that client programmers should pay attention to is 503 (Service Unavailable), which means that their request cannot be performed right now, but the Retry-After header (if supplied) indicates when the client might try again.

The following is a complete listing of response codes implying a server error:

Code	Meaning
500 Internal Server Error	This code indicates that a part of the server (for example, a CGI program) has crashed or encountered a configuration error.
501 Not Implemented	This code indicates that the client requested an action that cannot be performed by the server.

Code	Meaning
502 Bad Gateway	This code indicates that the server (or proxy) encountered invalid responses from another server (or proxy).
503 Service Unavailable	This code means that the service is temporarily unavailable, but should be restored in the future. If the server knows when it will be available again, a Retry-After header may also be supplied.
504 Gateway Time-out	This response is like 408 (Request Time-out) except that a gateway or proxy has timed out.
505 HTTP Version Not Supported	The server will not support the HTTP protocol version used in the request.

Headers

There are four types of HTTP headers:

- *General headers* indicate general information such as the date, or whether the connection should be maintained. They are used by both clients and servers.

- *Request headers* are used only for client requests. They convey the client's configuration and desired document format to the server.

- *Response headers* are used only in server responses. They describe the server's configuration and information about the requested URL.

- *Entity headers* describe the document format of the data being sent between client and server. Although Entity headers are most commonly used by the server when returning a requested document, they are also used by clients when using the POST or PUT methods.

Headers from all four categories may be specified in any order. Header names are case-insensitive, so the `Content-type` header is also frequently written as `Content-type`.

General Headers

General headers are used in both client requests and server responses. Some may be more specific to either a client or server message.

Cache-Control: *directives*

The `Cache-control` header specifies desired behavior from a caching system, as used in proxy servers. For example:

```
Cache-control: no-cache
```

Both clients and servers can use the `Cache-control` header to specify parameters for the cache or to request certain kinds of documents from the cache. The caching directives are specified in a comma-separated list.

Cache request directives are:

Directive	Meaning
`no-cache`	A cache can keep a cached copy of the document, but must always revalidate it before sending it back to the client.
`no-store`	Remove information promptly after forwarding. The cache should not store anything about the client request or server response. This option prevents the accidental storing of secure or sensitive information in the cache.
`max-age = seconds`	Do not send responses older than *seconds*. The cache can send a cached document that has been retrieved within a certain number of seconds from the time it was sent by the origin server.
`max-stale [ = seconds ]`	The cache can send a cached document that is older than its expiration date. If *seconds* are given, it must not be expired by more than that time.

Directive	Meaning
`min-fresh =` *seconds*	Send data only if still fresh after the specified number of seconds. The cache can send a cached document only if there are at least a certain number of seconds between now and its expiration time.
`only-if-` `cached`	Do not retrieve new data. The cache can send a document only if it is in the cache, and should not contact the origin-server to see if a newer copy exists. This option is useful when network connectivity from the cache to origin-server is poor.

Cache response directives are:

Directive	Meaning
`public`	The document is cacheable by any cache.
`private`	The document is not cacheable by a shared cache.
`no-cache`	A cache can keep a cached copy of the document, but must always revalidate it before sending it back to the client.
`no-store`	Do not store the returning document. Remove information promptly after forwarding.
`no-` `transform`	Do not convert the entity-body. Useful for applications that require that the message received is exactly what was sent by the server.
`must-` `revalidate`	The cache must verify the status of stale documents, i.e., the cache cannot blindly use a document that has expired.
`proxy-` `revalidate`	Client must revalidate data except for private client caches. Public caches must verify the status of stale documents. Like `must-revalidate`, excluding private caches.
`max-age =` *seconds*	The document should be considered stale in the specified number of seconds from the time of retrieval.
`s-maxage =` *seconds*	The same as `max-age`, except for public/shared caches. This directive is ignored by private caches.

Connection: *options*

Specifies options desired for this connection but not for further connections by proxies. For example:

```
Connection: close
```

The `close` option signifies that either the client or server wishes to end the connection (i.e., this is the last transaction). The `keep-alive` option signifies that the client wishes to keep the connection open. The default behavior of web applications differs between HTTP 1.0 and 1.1.

By default, HTTP 1.1 uses persistent connections, where the connection does not automatically close after a transaction. When an HTTP 1.1 web client no longer has any requests, or the server has reached some preprogrammed limit in spending resources on the client, a `Connection: close` header indicates that no more transactions will proceed, and the connection closes after the current one. An HTTP 1.1 client or server that doesn't support persistent connections should always use the `Connection: close` header.

HTTP 1.0, on the other hand, does not have persistent connections by default. If a 1.0 client wishes to use persistent connections, it uses the `keep-alive` parameter. A `Connection: keep-alive` header is issued by both HTTP 1.0 clients and servers for each transaction under persistent connections. The last transaction does not have a `Connection: keep-alive` header, and behaves like a `Connection: close` header under HTTP 1.1. HTTP 1.0 servers that do not support persistent connections will not have a `Connection: keep-alive` header in their response, and the client should disconnect after the first transaction completes.

Use of the `keep-alive` parameter is known to cause problems with proxy servers that do not understand persistent connections for HTTP 1.0. If a proxy server blindly forwards the `Connection: keep-alive` header, the origin-server and initial client are using persistent connections while the proxy server is not. The origin server maintains the network connection when the proxy server expects a disconnect; timing problems follow.

To get around that, when HTTP 1.1 proxies encounter an HTTP 1.0 request, it must remove the `Connection` header and any headers specified by the `Connection` header before forwarding the message.

Date: *dateformat*

There are three formats that can be used to express the date. The preferred date format is RFC 1123. For example:

```
Mon, 06 May 1996 04:57:00 GMT
```

The preferred RFC 1123 format specifies all dates in a fixed length string in Greenwich Mean Time (GMT). GMT is always used in HTTP to prevent any misunderstandings among computers communicating in different time zones. The valid days are: Mon, Tue, Wed, Thu, Fri, Sat, and Sun. The months are: Jan, Feb, Mar, Apr, May, Jun, Jul, Aug, Sep, Oct, Nov, and Dec.

For backwards compatibility, the RFC 1036 and ANSI C *asctime()* formats are also acceptable, but not recommended:

```
Monday, 06-May-96 04:57:00 GMT
Mon May 6 04:57:00 1996
```

The RFC 1036 format is similar to the one in RFC 1123, except that the string length varies, depending on the day of the week, and the year is specified in two digits instead of four. This makes date parsing more difficult. The valid days are: Monday, Tuesday, Wednesday, Thursday, Friday, Saturday, Sunday. The months are: Jan, Feb, Mar, Apr, May, Jun, Jul, Aug, Sep, Oct, Nov, and Dec.

ANSI C's *asctime()* format is not encouraged, since there can be misunderstandings about the time zone used by the computer. The valid days are: Mon, Tue, Wed, Thu, Fri, Sat, and Sun. The months are: Jan, Feb, Mar, Apr, May, Jun, Jul, Aug, Sep, Oct, Nov, and Dec.

Despite a heavy preference for RFC 1123's format, current web clients and servers should be able to recognize all three formats. However, when designing web programs, it is desirable to use RFC 1123 when generating dates. Future versions of HTTP may not support the latter two formats.

Pragma: *no-cache*

The Pragma header specifies directives for proxy and gateway systems. Since many proxy systems may exist between a client and server, Pragma headers must pass through each proxy. When the Pragma header reaches the server, the header may be ignored by the server software.

The only directive defined in HTTP/1.0 is the no-cache directive. It is used to tell caching proxies to contact the server for the requested document, instead of using its local cache. This allows the client to request the most up-to-date document from the original web server, without receiving a cached copy from an intermediate proxy server.

The Pragma header is an HTTP 1.0 feature, and is maintained in HTTP 1.1 for backward compatibility. No new Pragma directives will be defined in the future.

Example:

```
Pragma: no-cache
```

Trailer: *trailer_headers*

The Trailer header specifies the headers in the trailer of a chunked message. This header is not used if there are no headers specified after a chunked message. Also, it is not possible to expect Transfer-Encoding, Content-Length, or Trailer as a trailer header.

Transfer-Encoding: *encoding_type*

The Transfer-Encoding header specifies that the message is encoded. This is not the same as content-encoding (an entity-body header, discussed later), since transfer-encodings are a property of the message, not of the entity-body. For example:

```
Transfer-Encoding: chunked
```

In the HTTP 1.1 specification, chunked is the only encoding method supported.

The chunked transfer-encoding encodes the message as a series of chunks followed by entity-headers, as shown in Figure 6. The chunks and entity-headers are in a client's request entity-body or server response entity-body. Each chunk contains a chunk size specified in base 16, followed by CRLF. After that, the chunk body, whose length is specified in the chunk size, is presented, followed by a CRLF. Consecutive chunks are specified one after another, with the last chunk having a length of zero followed by CRLF. Entity-headers follow the chunks, terminated by a CRLF on a line by itself.

Entity-body

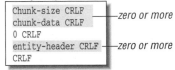

Figure 6. Chunked transfer encoding

Upgrade: *protocol/version*

Using the Upgrade header, the client can specify additional protocols that it understands, and that it would prefer to talk to the server with an alternate protocol. If the server wishes to use the alternate protocol, it returns a response code of 101 and indicates which protocol it is upgrading to, with the Upgrade header. After the terminating CRLF in the server's header response, the protocol switches.

Portion of client request:

    Upgrade: HTTP/1.2

Portion of server response:

    HTTP/1.1 101 Upgrading Protocols
    Upgrade: HTTP/1.2

Via: *protocol host*

The Via header is updated by proxy servers as messages pass from client to server and from server to client. Each proxy server appends its protocol and protocol version, hostname, port number, and comment to a comma-separated list on the Via header. If the Via header does not exist, the first proxy creates it. This information is useful for debugging purposes. If

---

the protocol name is HTTP, it can be omitted. For HTTP, a port number of 80 can be omitted. Comments are optional.

Example:

```
Via: 1.1 proxy.ora.com, 1.0 proxy.internic.gov
```

See the discussion of the TRACE method for more details.

Warning: *code host string*

Indicates information additional to that in the status code, for use by caching proxies. For example:

```
Warning: Response stale
```

The host field contains the name or pseudonym of the server host, with an optional port number. The two-digit warning codes and their recommended descriptive strings are:

Code	String	Meaning
110	Response stale	The response data is known to be stale.
111	Revalidation failed	The response data is known to be stale because the proxy failed to revalidate the data.
112	Disconnected operation	The cache is disconnected from the network.
113	Heuristic expiration	The data is older than 24 hours, and the cache heuristically chose a freshness lifetime greater than 24 hours.
199	Miscellaneous warning	Arbitrary information to be logged or presented to the user.
214	Transformation applied	The proxy has changed the encoding or media type of the document, as specified by the `Content-Encoding` or `Content-Type` headers.
299	Miscellaneous persistent warning	Arbitrary persistent information to be logged or presented to the user.

Client Request Headers

Client header data communicates the client's configuration and preferred document formats to the server. Request headers are used in a client message to provide information about the client.

Accept: *type/subtype [q=qvalue]*

Specifies media types the client prefers to accept. For example:

```
Accept: text/*, image/gif
```

Multiple media types can be listed separated by commas. The optional *qvalue* represents, on a scale of 0 to 1, an acceptable quality level for accept types.

Accept-Charset: *character_set [q=qvalue]*

Specifies the character sets that the client prefers. Multiple character sets can be listed separated by commas. The optional *qvalue* represents, on a scale of 0 to 1, an acceptable quality level for nonpreferred character sets. If this header is not specified, the server assumes the default of US-ASCII and ISO-8859-1 (a superset of US-ASCII), which are both specified in RFC 1521. For example:

```
Accept-charset: ISO-8859-7
```

Accept-Encoding: *encoding_types*

Through the Accept-Encoding header, a client may specify what encoding algorithms it understands. If this header is omitted, the server will send the requested entity-body without any additional encoding. Encoding mechanisms can be used to reduce consumption of scarce resources, at the expense of less expensive resources. For example, large files may be compressed to reduce transmission time over slow network connections.

In the HTTP/1.0 specification, two encoding mechanisms are defined: *x-gzip* and *x-compress*. Multiple encoding schemes can be listed, separated by commas. For reasons of compatibility

---

with historical practice, *gzip* and *compress* should be considered the same as *x-gzip* and *x-compress*.

Encoding Mechanism	Encoded By
gzip	Jean-Loup Gailly's GNU zip compression scheme
compress	Modified Lempel-Ziv compression scheme
deflate	The deflate method found in PKWARE products

For example:

```
Accept-encoding: gzip
```

There is no guarantee that the requested encoding mechanism has been applied to the entity-body returned by the server. If the client specifies an `Accept-encoding` header, it should examine the server's `Content-encoding` header to see if an encoding mechanism was applied. If the `Content-encoding` header has been omitted, no encoding mechanism was applied.

Accept-Language: *language [q=qvalue]*

Specifies the languages that the client prefers. If a client wants to specify a preference for a particular language, it is done in the `Accept-Language` header. If a server contains the same document in multiple languages, it will send the document in the language of the client's preference, when available. For example:

```
Accept-language: en
```

Multiple languages can be listed separated by commas. The optional `qvalue` represents, on a scale of 0 to 1, an acceptable quality level for nonpreferred languages. Languages are written with their two-letter abbreviations (e.g., `en` for English, `de` for German, `fr` for French, etc.).

Authorization: *scheme credentials*

Provides the client's authorization to access data at a URL. When a requested document requires authorization, the server returns a `WWW-Authenticate` header describing the type of authorization required. The client then repeats the request with the proper authorization information.

The HTTP/1.0 specification defines the BASIC authorization scheme, where the authorization parameter is the string of *username:password* encoded in base 64. For example, for the username of webmaster and a password of zrma4v, the authorization header would look like this:

    Authorization: BASIC d2VibWFzdGVyOnpycW1hNHY=

The value decodes into webmaster:zrma4v.

Cookie: *name=value*

Contains a name/value pair of information stored for that URL. For example:

    Cookie: acct=03847732

Multiple cookies can be specified, separated by semicolons. For browsers supporting cookies, see "Cookies" later in this book for more information.

An issue arises with proxy servers in regard to the headers. Set-Cookie and Cookie headers both should be propagated through the proxy, even if a page is cached or has not been modified (according to the If-Modified-Since condition). The Set-Cookie header should never be cached by the proxy.

Expect: *expectation*

This header indicates a client expectation about the server. If the server is not capable of the expectation, it returns a status code of 417 (Expectation Failed). The expectation must be met for all intermediate servers as well. All proxies, as well as the origin server must meet the expectation or return status code of 417.

From: *email_address*

Gives the email address of the user executing the client. The From header helps the server identify the source of malformed requests or excessive resource usage. For example:

    From: webmaster@www.ora.com

This header should be sent when possible, but should not be sent without the user's consent, in the interest of privacy.

However, when running clients that use excessive network or server resources, it is advisable to include this header, in the event that an administrator would like to contact the client user.

Host: *hostname:port*

The hostname and optional port number of the server contacted by the client. If the port number is 80, the colon and port number should be omitted. For example:

```
Host: www.ora.com
```

Or for a port number other than 80 (in this example, 7777):

```
Host: www.ora.com:7777
```

This is useful to indicate what server the client thinks it is talking to. It allows multihomed servers to use the same IP address with different DNS names. Clients must supply this information in HTTP 1.1, so servers with multiple hostnames can easily differentiate between ambiguous URLs.

If-Modified-Since: *date*

Specifies that the URL data is to be sent only if it has been modified since the date given as the value of this header. This is useful for client-side caching. For example:

```
If-Modified-Since: Mon, 04 May 1996 12:17:34 GMT
```

If the document has not been modified, the server returns a code of 304, indicating that the client should use the local copy. The specified date should follow the format described under the Date header.

If-Match: *entity_tag*

A conditional requesting the entity only if it matches the given entity tags (see the ETag entity header). An asterisk (*) matches any entity, and the transaction continues only if the entity exists.

If-None-Match: *entity_tag*

A conditional requesting the entity only if it does not match any of the given entity tags (see the ETag entity header). An asterisk (*) matches any entity; if the entity doesn't exist, the transaction continues.

If-Range: (*entity_tag* | *date*)

A conditional requesting only the portion of the entity that is missing, if it has not been changed, and the entire entity if it has. Used in conjunction with the Range header to indicate the entity tag or last modified time of a document on the server. For example:

```
If-Range: Mon, 04 May 1996 12:17:34 GMT
```

If the document has not been modified, the server returns the byte range given by the Range header; otherwise, it returns all of the new document. Either an entity tag or a date can be used to identify the partial entity already received; see the Date header for information on the format for dates.

If-Unmodified-Since: *date*

Specifies that the entity-body should be sent only if the document has not been modified since a given date. For example:

```
If-Unmodified-Since: Tue, 05 May 1996 04:03:56
GMT
```

The specified date should follow the format described under the Date header.

Max-Forwards: *n*

Limits the number of proxies or gateways that can forward the request. Useful for debugging with the TRACE method, avoiding infinite loops. For example:

```
Max-Forwards: 3
```

A proxy server that receives a Max-Forwards value of zero (0) should return the request headers to the client in its response entity-body. See the discussion of the TRACE method for more details.

Proxy-Authorization: *credentials*

For a client to identify itself to a proxy requiring authorization.

Range: bytes=*n-m*

Specifies the partial range(s) requested from the document. For example:

```
Range: bytes=1024-2047,4096-
```

Multiple ranges can be listed, separated by commas. If the first digit in the comma-separated byte range(s) is missing, the range is assumed to count from the end of the document. If the second digit is missing, the range is byte *n* to the end of the document. The first byte is byte 0.

Referer: *url*

Gives the URL of the document that refers to the requested URL (i.e., the source document of the link). For example:

```
Referer: http://www.yahoo.com/Internet/
```

TE: *transfer-codings*

This header specifies a comma separated list of the transfer-codings it is willing to accept. For example, to indicate that trailer fields in a chunked transfer-coding are acceptable:

```
TE: trailers
```

User-Agent: *string*

Gives identifying information about the client program. Here is an example:

```
User-Agent: Mozilla 3.0b
```

Server Response Headers

The response headers described here are used in server responses to communicate information about the server and how it may handle requests.

Accept-Ranges: bytes | none

Indicates the acceptance of range requests for a URL, specifying either the range unit (e.g., bytes) or none if no range requests are accepted. For example:

```
Accept-Ranges: bytes
```

Age: *seconds*

Indicates the age of the document in seconds. For example:

```
Age: 3521
```

ETag: *entity_tag*

This header specifies the entity tag for the requested server resource. The entity tag is a unique identifier associated with the server resource and can be used for caching purposes. The entity tag can then be used with the If-Match and If-None-Match request headers.

Location: *url*

Specifies the new location of a document, usually with response code 201 (Created), 301 (Moved Permanently), 302 (Found), 303 (See Other), or 307 (Moved Temporarily). The URL given must be written as an absolute URL. For example:

```
Location: http://www.ora.com/contacts.html
```

Proxy-Authenticate: *scheme realm*

Indicates the authentication scheme and parameters applicable to the proxy for this URL and the current connection. Used with response 407 (Proxy Authentication Required).

Retry-After: *date | seconds*

Specifies a time when the server can handle requests. Used with response code 503 (Service Unavailable). It contains either an integer number of seconds or a GMT date and time (as described by the Date header formats). If the value is an integer, it is interpreted as the number of seconds to wait after the request was issued. For example:

```
Retry-After: 3600
Retry-After: Sat, 18 May 1996 06:59:37 GMT
```

Server: *string*

Contains the name and version number of the server. For example:

```
Server: NCSA/1.3
```

Set-Cookie: *name=value options*

Contains a name/value pair of information to retain for this URL. For browsers supporting cookies. For example:

```
Set-Cookie: acct=03845324
```

Options are:

Option	Meaning
expires = *date*	The cookie becomes invalid after the specified date.
path = *pathname*	The URL range for which the cookie is valid.
domain = *domain_name*	The domain name range for which the cookie is valid.
secure	Return the cookie only under a secure connection.

Vary: *headers*

Specifies that the entity has multiple sources and may therefore vary according to specified list of request header(s).

```
Vary: Accept-Language,Accept-Encoding
```

Multiple headers can be listed, separated by commas. An asterisk (*) means that another factor, other than the request headers, may affect the document that is returned.

WWW-Authenticate: *scheme realm*

A request for authentication, used with the 401 (Unauthorized) response code. It specifies the authorization scheme and realm of authorization required from a client at the requested URL. Many different authorization realms can exist on a server. A common authorization scheme is BASIC, which requires a username and password. For example:

```
WWW-Authenticate: BASIC realm="Admin"
```

When returned to the client, this header indicates that the BASIC type of authorization data in the appropriate realm should be returned in the client's Authorization header.

Another scheme is *Digest*, which improves security by not transmitting the password as cleartext. The BASIC and Digest schemes are described in RFC 2617. Unfortunately, Digest is not widely used, given that not all browsers support it.

Windows-based HTTP servers sometimes use a scheme called *NTLM*. It isn't as widely used as BASIC as well, given that not all browsers implement the NTLM scheme.

Entity Headers

Entity headers are used in both client requests and server responses. They supply information about the entity body in an HTTP message.

Allow: *methods*

Contains a comma-separated list of methods that are allowed at a specified URL. In a server response it is used with code 405 (Method Not Allowed) to inform the client of valid methods available for the requested information. For example:

```
Allow: GET, HEAD
```

Some methods may not apply to a URL, and the server must verify that the methods supplied by the client makes sense with the given URL.

Content-Encoding: *encoding_schemes*

Specifies the encoding scheme(s) used for the transferred entity-body. Values are *gzip* (or *x-gzip*) and *compress* (or *x-compress*). If multiple encoding schemes are specified (in a comma-separated list), they must be listed in the order in which they were applied to the source data.

The server should attempt to use an encoding scheme used by the client's Accept-Encoding header. The client may use this information to determine how to decode the document after it is transferred.

See the description of the Accept-Encoding header earlier in this appendix for a listing of possible values. For example:

```
Content-Encoding: x-gzip
```

Content-Language: *languages*

Specifies the language(s) that the transferred entity-body is intended for. Languages are represented by their two-letter abbreviations (e.g., en for English, fr for French). The server should attempt to use a language specified by the client's Accept-Language header. This header is useful when a client specifies a preference for one language over another for a given URL. For example:

```
Content-Language: fr
```

Content-Length: *n*

This header specifies the length of the data (in bytes) of the transferred entity-body. For example:

```
Content-Length:  47293
```

Due to the dynamic nature of some requests, the content length is sometimes unknown and this header is omitted.

Content-Location: *url*

Supplies the URL for the entity, in cases where a document has multiple entities with separately accessible locations. The URL can be either an absolute or relative URL. For example:

```
Content-Location: http://www.ora.com/products/
```

See the section "Retrieving Content" later in this book.

Content-MD5: *digest*

Supplies an MD5 digest of the entity, for checking the integrity of the message upon receipt. For example:

```
Content-MD5: d41d8cd98f00b204e9800998ecf8427e
```

Content-Range: bytes *n-n/m*

Specifies where the accompanying partial entity-body should be inserted, and the total size of the full entity-body. For example:

```
Content-Range: bytes 6143-7166/15339
```

Content-Type: *type/subtype*

Describes the media type and subtype of an entity-body. It uses the same values as the client's Accept header, and the server should return media types that conform with the client's preferred formats. For example:

```
Content-type: text/html
```

Expires: *date*

Specifies the time when a document may change, or when its information becomes invalid. After that time, the document may or may not change or be deleted. The value is a date and time in a valid format as described for the Date header. For example:

```
Expires: Sat, 20 May 1995 03:32:38 GMT
```

This is useful for cache management. The Expires header means it is unlikely that the document will change before the given time. This does not imply that the document will be changed or deleted at that time. It is only an advisory that the document will not be modified until the specified time.

Last-Modified: *date*

Specifies when the URL was last modified. The value is a date and time in a valid format as described for the Date header. If a client has a copy of the URL in its cache that is older than the last-modified date, it should be refreshed. For example:

```
Last-Modified: Sat, 20 May 1995 03:32:38 GMT
```

Summary of Support Across HTTP Versions

The following is a listing of all HTTP headers supported by each version of HTTP so far.

HTTP 0.9

Method	General	Request	Entity	Response
GET	None	None	None	None

HTTP 1.0

Method	General	Request	Entity	Response
GET	Connection	Accept	Allow	Location
HEAD	Date	Accept-charset	Content-encoding	Retry-after
POST	MIME-version	Accept-encoding	Content-language	Server
PUT	Pragma	Accept-language	Content-length	WWW-Authenticate
DELETE		Authorization	Content-type	
LINK		From	Expires	
UNLINK		If-modified-since	Last-modified	
		Referer	Link	
		User-agent	Title	
			URL	

HTTP 1.1

Method	General	Request	Entity	Response
OPTIONS	Cache-control	Accept	Allow	Accept-Ranges
GET	Connection	Accept-charset	Content-encoding	Age
HEAD	Date	Accept-encoding	Content-language	Etag
POST	Pragma	Accept-language	Content-length	Location
PUT	Trailer	Authorization	Content-location	Proxy-authenticate
DELETE	Transfer-encoding	Expect	Content-md5	Retry-after
TRACE	Upgrade	From	Content-range	Server
CONNECT	Via	Host	Content-type	Vary

Method	General	Request	Entity	Response
	Warning	If-modified-since	Expires	WWW-Authenticate
		If-match	Last-modified	
		If-none-match		
		If-range		
		If-unmodified-since		
		Max-forwards		
		Proxy-authorization		
		Range		
		Referer		
		TE		
		User-agent		

URL Encoding

When the client sends data to a CGI program using the Content-type of *application/x-www-form urlencoded*, certain special characters are encoded to eliminate ambiguity. Table 1 shows which characters are transformed and which are not transformed. For more information on URLs, see RFC 1738.

Table 1. Character Encoding

ASCII	Symbol	CGI Representation
< 32		*Always encode with %xx where xx is the hexadecimal representation of the character*
32		+ or %20
33	!	%21
34	"	%22
35	#	%23

Table 1. Character Encoding (continued)

ASCII	Symbol	CGI Representation
36	$	%24
37	%	%25
38	&	%26
39	'	%27
40	(	%28
41	)	%29
42	*	*
43	+	%2B
44	,	%2C
45	-	-
46	.	.
47	/	%2F
48	0	0
49	1	1
50	2	2
51	3	3
52	4	4
53	5	5
54	6	6
55	7	7
56	8	8
57	9	9
58	:	%3A
59	;	%3B
60	<	%3C
61	=	%3D
62	>	%3E
63	?	%3F
64	@	%40
65	A	A
66	B	B
67	C	C

Table 1. Character Encoding (continued)

ASCII	Symbol	CGI Representation
68	D	D
69	E	E
70	F	F
71	G	G
72	H	H
73	I	I
74	J	J
75	K	K
76	L	L
77	M	M
78	N	N
79	O	O
80	P	P
81	Q	Q
82	R	R
83	S	S
84	T	T
85	U	U
86	V	V
87	W	W
88	X	X
89	Y	Y
90	Z	Z
91	[	%5B
92	\	%5C
93	]	%5D
94	^	%5E
95	_	_
96	`	%60
97	a	a
98	b	b
99	c	c

Table 1. Character Encoding (continued)

ASCII	Symbol	CGI Representation
100	d	d
101	e	e
102	f	f
103	g	g
104	h	h
105	i	i
106	j	j
107	k	k
108	l	l
109	m	m
110	n	n
111	o	o
112	p	p
113	q	q
114	r	r
115	s	s
116	t	t
117	u	u
118	v	v
119	w	w
120	x	x
121	y	y
122	z	z
123	{	%7B
124	|	%7C
125	}	%7D
126	~	%7E
127		%7F
> 127		*Always encode with %xx where xx is the hexadecimal representation of the character*

The remainder of this book presents an overview of how certain HTTP functionality is performed using the appropriate headers and status codes.

Client and Server Identification

Clients and servers can optionally identify themselves. Clients send a User-agent header and servers sent the Server header. Even though these headers are optional, the protocol specification encourages their use. Some benefits are:

- Servers can respond with customized content for a particular client. Such customized content may work around a bug in a particular version of a browser, or may make use of advanced features in more modern browsers when possible.

- Surveys and statistics collections of browser and server deployment.

- Tracking of client or server software that violates the HTTP specification.

However, when a server identifies itself, there is some security risk, given that a user now knows the type of server and may be able to apply security exploits for a known vulnerability on a particular version of the server software. In light of this, some web servers are configured to not display the Server header.

Referring Documents

The Referer header indicates which document referred to the one currently specified in this request. This helps the server keep track of documents that refer to malformed or missing locations on the server.

For example, if the client opens a connection to *www.ora.com* at port 80 and sends:

```
GET /contact.html HTTP/1.1
Host: www.ora.com
```

The server may respond with:

```
HTTP/1.1 200 OK
Date: Tue, 04 Apr 2000 02:22:47 GMT
Last-Modified: Sat, 18 Mar 2000 17:18:22 GMT
ETag: "134e8-b2a-38d3ba5e"
Accept-Ranges: bytes
Content-Length: 2858
Connection: close
Content-type: text/html

<h1>Contact Information</h1>
<a href="http://sales.ora.com/sales.html">
Sales Department</a>
```

The user clicks on the hyperlink and the client requests *sales.html* from *sales.ora.com*, specifying that it was sent there from the */contact.html* document on *www.ora.com*:

```
GET /sales.html HTTP/1.1
Host: sales.ora.com
Referer: http://www.ora.com/contact.html
```

Retrieving Content

The Content-length header specifies the length of the data (in bytes) that is returned by the server. Due to the dynamic nature of some requests, the Content-length is sometimes unknown, and this header might be omitted.

There are three common ways that a client can retrieve data from the entity-body of the server's response:

- The first method involves retrieving the size of the document from the Content-length header, and then reading in that much data from the network connection. Using this method, the client knows the size of the document before retrieving it.

- In other cases, when the size of the document is too dynamic for a server to predict, the `Content-length` header is omitted. When this happens, the client reads in the data portion of the server's response until the server disconnects the network connection. This practice is obsolete and only works in HTTP 1.0. For generating data without knowing the total message length in advance, the next method is recommended.

- Another header could indicate when an entity-body ends, like HTTP 1.1's `Transfer-Encoding` header with the `chunked` parameter.

Byte Ranges

In HTTP 1.1, the client does not have to retrieve the entire entity-body at once, but can get it in pieces, if the server allows it to do so. If the server declares that it supports byte ranges using the `Accept-Ranges` header:

```
HTTP/1.1 200 OK
[Other headers here]
Accept-Ranges: bytes
```

The client can then request the data in pieces. For example:

```
GET /largefile.html HTTP/1.1
[Other headers here]
Range: 0-65535
```

When the server returns the specified range, it includes a `Content-range` header to indicate which portion of the document is being sent, and also to tell the client how long the file is:

```
HTTP/1.1 200 OK
[Other headers here]
Content-range: 0-65535/83028576
```

For caching purposes, a client can use the `If-Range` header along with `Range` to request an updated portion of the document only if the document has been changed. Here is an example:

```
GET /largefile.html HTTP/1.1
[Other headers here]
If-Range: Mon, 02 May 1996 04:51:00 GMT
Range: 0-65535
```

The If-Range header can use either a last modified date or an entity tag to verify that the document is still the same.

Media Types

One of the most important functions of headers is to make it possible for the recipient of the data to know what kind of data it is receiving, and thus be able to process it appropriately. If the client didn't know that the data returned by the server was a GIF image, it wouldn't know how to render it on the screen. If it didn't know that some other data was an audio snippet, it wouldn't know to call up an external helper application. For negotiating different data types, HTTP incorporated Internet Media Types, which look a lot like MIME types but are not exactly MIME types.

The client tells the server which media types it can handle, using the Accept header. The server tries to return information in one of the client's preferred media types, and declares the type of the data using the Content-type header.

The Accept header is used to specify the client's preference for media formats, or to tell the server that it can accept unusual document types. If this header is omitted, the server assumes that the client can accept any media type. The Accept header can have three general forms:

```
Accept: */*
Accept: type/*
Accept: type/subtype
```

Using the first form, */*, indicates that the client can accept an entity-body of any media type. The second form, type/*, communicates that an entity-body of a certain general class is acceptable. A client may issue an `Accept: image/*` to accept images, where the type of image (GIF, JPEG, or whatever) is not important. The third form indicates that an entity-body from a certain type and subtype is acceptable. For example, a browser that can only accept GIF files may use `Accept: image/gif`.

The client specifies multiple document types that it can accept by separating the values with commas:

```
Accept: image/gif, image/x-xbitmap, image/
jpeg, image/pjpeg, */*
```

Some older browsers send the same line as:

```
Accept: image/gif
Accept: image/x-xbitmap
Accept: image/jpeg
Accept: image/pjpeg
Accept: */*
```

When developing a new application, it is recommended that it conform to the newer practice of separating multiple document preferences by commas, with a single `Accept` header.

In the server's response, the `Content-type` header describes the type and subtype of the media. If the client specified an `Accept` header, the media type should conform to the values used in the `Accept` header. Clients use this information to correctly handle the media type and format of the entity body.

A client might also use a `Content-type` header with the POST or PUT method. Most commonly, with many CGI applications, clients use a POST or PUT request with information in the entity-body, and supply a `Content-type` header to describe what data can be expected in the entity-body.

Table 2 lists commonly used media types, along with the filename suffixes that are recognized by most servers. These servers can be easily configured to recognize additional suffixes as well.

Table 2. Internet Media Types

Type/Subtype	Usual Extension
application/activemessage	
application/andrew-inset	
application/applefile	
application/atomicmail	
application/cals-1840	
application/commonground	
application/cybercash	
application/dca-rft	
application/dec-dx	
application/EDI-Consent	
application/EDIFACT	
application/EDI-X12	
application/eshop	
application/hyperstudio	
application/iges	
application/mac-binhex40	
application/macwriteii	
application/marc	
application/mathematica	
application/msword	*doc*
application/news-message-id	
application/news-transmission	
application/octet-stream	*bin*
application/oda	*oda*
application/pdf	*pdf*
application/pgp-encrypted	
application/pgp-signature	
application/pgp-keys	

Table 2. Internet Media Types (continued)

Type/Subtype	Usual Extension
application/pkcs7-mime	
application/pkcs7-signature	
application/pkcs10	
application/postscript	*ai, eps, ps*
application/prs.alvestrand.titrax-sheet	
application/prs.cww	
application/prs.nprend	
application/remote-printing	
application/riscos	
application/rtf	*rtf*
application/set-payment-initiation	
application/set-payment	
application/set-registration-initiation	
application/set-registration	
application/sgml	*sgm, sgml, gml, dtd*
application/sgml-open-catalog	*soc, cat*
application/slate	
application/vemmi	
application/vnd.$commerce_battelle	
application/vnd.3M Post-it Notes	
application/vnd.acucobol	
application/vnd.anser-web-funds-transfer-initiation	
application/vnd.anser-web-certificate-issue-initiation	
application/vnd.audiograph	
application/vnd.businessobjects	
application/vnd.claymore	

Table 2. Internet Media Types (continued)

Type/Subtype	Usual Extension
application/vnd.comsocaller	
application/vnd.dna	
application/vnd.dxr	
application/vnd.ecdis-update	
application/vnd.ecowin.chart	
application/vnd.ecowin.filerequest	
application/vnd.ecowin.fileupdate	
application/vnd.ecowin.series	
application/vnd.ecowin.seriesrequest	
application/vnd.ecowin.seriesupdate	
application/vnd.enliven	
application/vnd.epson.salt	
application/vnd.fdf	
application/vnd.ffsns	
application/vnd.FloGraphIt	
application/vnd.framemaker	
application/vnd.fujitsu.oasys	
application/vnd.fujitsu.oasys2	
application/vnd.fujitsu.oasys3	
application/vnd.fujitsu.oasysprs	
application/vnd.fujitsu.oasysgp	
application/vnd.fujixerox.docuworks	
application/vnd.hp-hps	
application/vnd.hp-HPGL	
application/vnd.hp-PCL	
application/vnd.hp-PCLXL	
application/vnd.ibm.MiniPay	
application/vnd.ibm.modcap	

Table 2. Internet Media Types (continued)

Type/Subtype	Usual Extension
application/vnd.intercon.formnet	
application/vnd.intertrust.digibox	
application/vnd.intertrust.nncp	
application/vnd.is-xpr	
application/vnd.japannet-directory-service	
application/vnd.japannet-jpnstore-wakeup	
application/vnd.japannet-payment-wakeup	
application/vnd.japannet-registration	
application/vnd.japannet-registration-wakeup	
application/vnd.japannet-setstore-wakeup	
application/vnd.japannet-verification	
application/vnd.japannet-verification-wakeup	
application/vnd.koan	
application/vnd.lotus-wordpro	
application/vnd.lotus-approach	
application/vnd.lotus-1-2-3	
application/vnd.lotus-organizer	
application/vnd.lotus-screencam	
application/vnd.lotus-freelance	
application/vnd.meridian slingshot	
application/vnd.mif	
application/vnd.minisoft-hp3000-save	
application/vnd.mitsubishi.misty-guard.trustweb	

Table 2. Internet Media Types (continued)

Type/Subtype	Usual Extension
application/vnd.ms-artgalry	
application/vnd.ms-asf	
application/vnd.ms-excel	
application/vnd.ms-powerpoint	
application/vnd.ms-project	
application/vnd.ms-tnef	
application/vnd.ms-works	
application/vnd.music-niff	
application/vnd.musician	
application/vnd.netfpx	
application/vnd.noblenet-web	
application/vnd.noblenet-sealer	
application/vnd.noblenet-directory	
application/vnd.novadigm.EDM	
application/vnd.novadigm.EDX	
application/vnd.novadigm.EXT	
application/vnd.osa.netdeploy	
application/vnd.powerbuilder6	
application/vnd.powerbuilder6-s	
application/vnd.rapid	
application/vnd.seemail	
application/ vnd.shana.informed.formtemplate	
application/vnd.shana.informed.form-data	
application/ vnd.shana.informed.package	
application/vnd.shana.informed.interchange	

Table 2. Internet Media Types (continued)

Type/Subtype	Usual Extension
application/vnd.street-stream	
application/vnd.svd	
application/vnd.swiftview-ics	
application/vnd.truedoc	
application/vnd.visio	
application/vnd.webturbo	
application/vnd.wrq-hp3000-labelled	
application/vnd.wt.stf	
application/vnd.xara	
application/vnd.yellowriver-custom-menu	
application/wita	
application/wordperfect5.1	
application/x-bcpio	*bcpio*
application/x-cpio	*cpio*
application/x-csh	*csh*
application/x-dvi	*dvi*
application/x-gtar	*gtar*
application/x-hdf	*hdf*
application/x-latex	*latex*
application/x-mif	*mif*
application/x-netcdf	*nc, cdf*
application/x-sh	*sh*
application/x-shar	*shar*
application/x-sv4cpio	*sv4cpio*
application/x-sv4crc	*sv4crc*
application/x-tar	*tar*
application/x-tcl	*tcl*
application/x-tex	*tex*

Table 2. Internet Media Types (continued)

Type/Subtype	Usual Extension
application/x-texinfo	*texinfo, texi*
application/x-troff-man	*man*
application/x-troff-me	*me*
application/x-troff-ms	*ms*
application/x-troff	*t, tr, roff*
application/x-ustar	*ustar*
application/x-wais-source	*src*
application/xml	*xml, dtd*
application/x400-bp	
application/zip	*zip*
audio/32kadpcm	
audio/32kadpcm	
audio/basic	*au, snd*
audio/vnd.qcelp	*wav*
audio/x-aiff	*aif, aiff, aifc*
audio/x-wav	*wav*
image/cgm	*cgm*
image/g3fax	
image/gif	*gif*
image/ief	*ief*
image/jpeg	*jpeg, jpg, jpe*
image/naplps	
image/png	*png*
image/tiff	*tiff, tif*
image/vnd.dwg	
image/vnd.dxf	
image/vnd.fpx	
image/vnd.net-fpx	

Table 2. Internet Media Types (continued)

Type/Subtype	Usual Extension
image/vnd.svf	
image/vnd.xiff	
image/x-cmu-raster	*ras*
image/x-portable-anymap	*rpnm*
image/x-portable-bitmap	*pbm*
image/x-portable-graymap	*pgm*
image/x-portable-pixmap	*ppm*
image/x-rgb	*rgb*
image/x-xbitmap	*xbm*
image/x-xpixmap	*xpm*
image/x-xwindowdump	*xwd*
message/external-body	
message/http	
message/news	
message/partial	
message/rfc822	
model/iges	
model/mesh	
model/vnd.dwf	
model/vrml	
multipart/alternative	
multipart/appledouble	
multipart/digest	
multipart/form-data	
multipart/header-set	
multipart/mixed	
multipart/parallel	
multipart/related	

Table 2. Internet Media Types (continued)

Type/Subtype	Usual Extension
multipart/report	
multipart/voice-message	
text/enriched	
text/html	*html, htm*
text/plain	*txt*
text/richtext	*rtx*
text/sgml	*sgm, sgml, gml, dtd*
text/tab-separated-values	*tsv*
text/xml	*xml, dtd*
text/x-setext	*etx*
video/mpeg	*mpeg, mpg, mpe*
video/quicktime	*qt, mov*
video/vnd.vivo	
video/vnd.motorola.video	
video/vnd.motorola.videop	
video/x-msvideo	*qvi*
video/x-sgi-movie	*movie*

Cookies

Cookies allow web servers to store state information in the browser. They are often used to store session variables, user preferences, or user identity. Cookies are not part of the HTTP specification; however, they have become ubiquitous and are sometimes needed for proper interactions with some web sites.

Cookies work in the following way: when a server program wishes to store state information in the client, the server issues a `Set-Cookie` header its response to the client, which contains the value it wishes to store. The client is expected to store the information from the Set-Cookie header, associated with the URL or domain that issues the cookie. In subsequent requests to that URL or domain, the client should include the cookie information using the Cookie header. The server or CGI program uses this information to return a document tailored to that specific client. The server can set an expiration date for the cookie, or just use it for a session that will not survive beyond the current instance of the browser.

For example, the client may fill in a form opening a new account. The request might read:

```
POST /sales.ora.com/order.pl HTTP/1.0
[Client headers here]

type=new&firstname=John&lastname=Smith
```

The server stores this information along with a new account ID, and sends it back in the response:

```
HTTP/1.0 200 OK
[Server headers here]
Set-Cookie:
acct=04382374;domain=.ora.com;Expires=Sun, 16-
Feb-2003 04:38:14 GMT;Path=/
```

The next time the browser visits the site, the client should recognize that a cookie is needed, and send:

```
GET /order.pl HTTP/1.0
[Client headers here]
Cookie: acct=04382374
```

More details about cookies are available at:

```
http://www.netscape.com/newsref/std/cookie_
spec.html
```

Authorization

An Authorization header is used to request restricted documents. Upon first requesting a restricted document, the

---

web client requests the document without sending an Authorization header. If the server denies access to the document, the server specifies the authorization method for the client to use with the WWW-Authenticate header. At this point, the client requests the document again, but with an Authorization header.

The Authorization header is of the general form:

```
Authorization: SCHEME REALM
```

The authorization scheme generally used in HTTP is BASIC, and under the BASIC scheme the credentials follow the format *username:password* encoded in base 64. For example, for the username of webmaster and a password of zrqma4v, the Authorization header would look like this:

```
Authorization: Basic d2VibWFzdGVyOnpycW1hNHY=
```

When d2VibWFzdGVyOnpycW1hNHY= is decoded using base 64, it translates into webmaster:zrqma4v.

For example, a client requests information that requires authorization, and the server responds with response code 401 (Unauthorized) and an appropriate WWW-Authenticate header describing the type of authentication required:

```
GET /sample.html HTTP/1.0
User-Agent: Mozilla/1.1N (Macintosh; I; 68K)
Accept: */*
Accept: image/gif
Accept: image/x-xbitmap
Accept: image/jpeg
```

The server then declares that further authorization is required to access the URL:

```
HTTP/1.0 401 Unauthorized
Date: Sat, 20-May-95 03:32:38 GMT
Server: NCSA/1.3
MIME-version: 1.0
Content-type: text/html
WWW-Authenticate:  BASIC realm="System
Administrator"
```

The client now seeks authentication information. Interactive GUI-based browsers might prompt the user for a user name and password in a dialog box. Other clients might just get the information from an online file or a hardware device.

The realm of the authentication scheme indicates the type of authentication requested. Each realm is defined by the web administrator of the site and indicates a class of users: administrators, CGI programmers, registered users, or anything else that separates one class of authorization from another. After encoding the data appropriately for the BASIC authorization method, the client resends the request with proper authorization:

```
GET /sample.html HTTP/1.0
User-Agent: Mozilla/1.1N (Macintosh; I; 68K)
Accept: */*
Accept: image/gif
Accept: image/x-xbitmap
Accept: image/jpeg
Authorization: BASIC d2VibWFzdGVyOnpycWW1hNHY=
```

The server checks the authorization, and upon successful authentication, sends the requested data:

```
HTTP/1.0 200 OK
Date: Sat, 20-May-95 03:25:12 GMT
Server: NCSA/1.3
MIME-version: 1.0
Content-type: text/html
Last-modified: Wednesday, 14-Mar-95 18:15:23
GMT
Content-length: 1029

[Entity-body data]
```

There's also something called *Digest* authentication. The Digest authentication scheme provides security benefits over the BASIC scheme. Unfortunately, the major web browsers do not support it, and web sites tend not to make use of it for this reason. There are some HTTP client libraries that

---

make use of it, however. See RFC 2617 for more information about the Digest format.

Persistent Connections

A major feature required in HTTP 1.1 is persistent connections. Persistent connections keep the network connection open for multiple transactions between the client and server to occur. Under both HTTP 1.0 and 1.1, the *Connection* header controls whether or not the network connection stays open; however, its use varies according to the version of HTTP.*

The Connection header indicates whether the network connection will be maintained after the current transaction finishes. The close parameter signifies that either the client or server wishes to end the connection (i.e., this is the last transaction). The keep-alive parameter signifies that the client wishes to keep the connection open. Under HTTP 1.0, the default is to close connections after each transaction, so the client must use the following header in order to maintain the connection for an additional request:

```
Connection: Keep-Alive
```

Under HTTP 1.1, the default is to keep connections open until they are explicitly closed. The keep-alive option is therefore unnecessary under HTTP 1.1; however, clients must be sure to include the following header in their last transaction:

```
Connection: Close
```

or the connection will remain open until the server times out the connection. How long it takes the server to time out depends on the server's configuration; but needless to say, it's more considerate to close the connection explicitly.

---

* Persistent connections are not in the HTTP 1.0 specification, but it was common practice for HTTP 1.0 software to implement persistent connections.

Client Caching

To reduce bandwidth usage and latency, clients are encouraged to cache the data retrieved from a web server.

On sites with proxy servers, the proxy can also work as a cache. This allows a user of the proxy server to use documents that might have been previously retrieved and cached by other users of the proxy.

A complication with caching, however, is that the client or proxy needs to know when the document has changed on the server. HTTP provides a mechanism for cache management through a set of headers. There are two general methods for determining if a server resource has changed. One method checks for the most recent modification time of the document. Another method checks for modifications in the entity tag associated with the document.

The server can also use the `Cache-Control` and `Pragma` headers to indicate caching properties to the client. Some documents aren't appropriate for caching, either for security reasons or because they are dynamic documents (e.g., created on the fly by a CGI script). Under HTTP 1.0, the `Pragma` header with a `no-cache` value indicates the document should not be cached. Under HTTP 1.1, the `Cache-Control` header supplants `Pragma`, with several caching directives in addition to `no-cache`.

If-Modified-Since

To accommodate client-side caching of documents, the client can use the `If-Modified-Since` header with the GET method. When using this option, the client requests the server to send the requested information associated with the URL only if it has been modified since a client-specified time.

If the document was modified, the server will give a status code of 200 and returns the document in the entity-body of its reply. If the document was not modified, the server will give a response code of 304 (Not Modified).

An example If-Modified-Since header might read:

```
If-Modified-Since: Fri, 02-Jun-95 02:42:43 GMT
```

If the server returns a code of 304, the document has not been modified since the specified time. The client can use the cached version of the document. If the document is newer, the server will send it along with a 200 (OK) code. Servers may also include a Last-Modified header with the document, to let the user know when the last change was made to the document.

Another related client header is If-Unmodified-Since, which says to only send the document if it *hasn't* been changed since the specified date. This is useful for ensuring that the data is exactly the way you wanted it to be. For example, if you GET a document from a server, make changes in a publishing tool, and PUT it back to the server, you can use the If-Unmodified-Since header to verify that the changes you made are accepted by the server only if the previous one you were looking at is still there.

If the server contains an Expires header, this indicates the document will not change before the time specified in the header. Although there are no guarantees, it means that the client does not have to ask the server about the last modified date of the document again until after the expiration date.

Entity Tags

In HTTP 1.1, a new method of cache management involves *entity tags*. The problem solved by entity tags is that there may be several copies of the same document on the server. The client has no way of knowing that it's the same document—so even if it the client already has a copy of the document, the client will request the document again.

Entity tags are unique identifiers that can be associated with all copies of the document. If the document changes, the entity tag changes—so it is more efficient to check for the entity tag, not for the URL and `Last-Modified` date.

If the server uses entity tags, it sends the document with the `ETag` header. When the client wants to verify if a document matches a particular entity tag, it uses the `If-Match` or `If-None-Match` header.